GEORGES
ROUAULT

MISERERE

WITH A PREFACE
BY THE ARTIST

AND AN INTRODUCTION
BY MONROE WHEELER

THE MUSEUM OF MODERN ART NEW YORK

The original edition of Miserere *was published in 1948 by Editions de l'Etoile Filante, 21 Boulevard St. Germain, Paris. It was limited to 450 copies of which twenty-five were not for sale.*

The gravure illustrations in this volume were printed in Paris by the master-printer Aulard, under the supervision of the artist, for Arnold Fawcus of the Grey Falcon Press of Paris and New York.

The typography of this edition is by Edward Lloyd Mills. The text was printed by The John B. Watkins Company, New York.

Library of Congress Catalog Card Number 52-8813

INTRODUCTION BY MONROE WHEELER

A predominant characteristic of Georges Rouault, the man and the artist, is his unwavering and almost violent ardor, not only in his practice of art, but in his moral persuasions and religious faith. The story of his life is clarified when we consider it in this light. In his teens, apprenticed to a stained-glass maker, when he was given omnibus fare for an errand on the other side of Paris, he would run along beside the vehicle in order to keep the few sous for himself to buy drawing paper, with no loss of time or money to his employer. And when his long work-day was over, he would again walk the breadth of Paris and back, to attend an art class. These little incidents are indicative of the steadfastness which he has maintained until his present age of eighty.

Almost all his life-work was conceived in his young manhood, and never deviated from, except for the enrichment of his means of pictorial expression. Canvas after canvas was begun, and put away, and undertaken again and again, with an obstinacy that has become proverbial in modern art.

The volume here reproduced in small facsimile was conceived by Rouault at the very beginning of the first world war. At first two volumes, with a total of one hundred plates, were projected, one to be called *Miserere,* the other *Guerre;* and Ambroise Vollard agreed to finance and publish both. Long afterward, when fifty-eight plates had been completed, it was announced that they would appear under the title of *Miserere et Guerre* and, as proofs of the plates were circulated and exhibited, there are many printed references to this name. Vollard died in 1939, and this caused a further delay while the claims of heirs were being established. In 1948, having passed back into Rouault's hands, they were at last issued by L'Etoile Filante, in Paris, in an edition of

450 copies. At this time the title was reduced to the one word, *Miserere*. The present volume has been produced at Rouault's own wish and under his personal supervision, not only to spread the enjoyment of his art, but to convey to a new and larger public the religious message which means so much to him.

Thirteen years passed between Rouault's first drawings for the plates in 1914, and their final printing in 1927; twenty-one more years elapsed before their publication. The story of this long interlude, and of Rouault's relations with his dealer and publisher, Vollard, is not easy to relate or clarify. An underlying appreciation and loyalty held the two men together, despite quarrels which were notable for the fierceness with which Rouault resisted any deviation from the true course of his artistic inspiration, any haste or compromise. Nor did Vollard, for his part, desist from other ventures which led him to defer the publication of *Miserere*.

To this day, Rouault, pacing up and down his Paris apartment, fierily discourses on the vicissitudes of his art, the inspiration and successive stages of the present volume, his difficulties with Vollard, and his experimentations with the graphic media. He makes one think of an old soldier as he recalls his combativity of the past, or of a pioneer or an explorer in his proud account of his innovations.

He has summed it up for us in his own foreword which follows. After the first drawings were made, at Vollard's order they were transformed into paintings, in gouache or oil. It was upon Vollard's initiative also, that the subjects were then photo-engraved upon the largest copper plates that the etching press could accommodate — 21 by 18 inches being the average size. These were given to Rouault for further development. Doubtless this was intended to facilitate his creative labor, but Rouault states that it had the opposite effect. He wishes that he himself had worked upon the copper from the beginning; he would not then have been constrained to obliterate and rework by hand all the parts of the original design which were ineffectual on metal. "They gave me back the copper," he says, "and I just dug into it."

For five years, from 1922 to 1927, in obsession, delight and despair, he worked at perfecting the *Miserere* plates, usually afternoons and evenings, sometimes three full days a week; the rest of the time he continued his painting. Always contemptuous of facility, he made as many as fifteen successive states of a single subject, using whatever combination of techniques would bring the result he desired: aquatint, drypoint, roulette, and direct application of acid with a brush. It is apparent, however, that in some places the photo-engraving produced remarkable effects which handwork alone might not have attained. On the reverse of plate 58, four states of one print show how the artist achieved that mystic brilliance and intensity which is unique in modern art. After all the plates had been printed by the master-printer, Jacquemin, Vollard announced that they would appear with a more or less devotional text to be written by André Suarès, but this was never forthcoming.

What Rouault has now given to us and to posterity is a set of magnificent plates, an album, with no text save a brief foreword by himself and a caption for each plate. There is a tradition in Catholicism and in the cultural history of Europe for such unliterary books, intended for the edification and uplift of those who could read only a little, or not at all. Inheriting the spirit and iconography of the late middle ages, this album takes its place in the first rank of twentieth-century art; and in the particular category of modern religious art, it is perhaps the greatest single work.

From the beginning of his life, Rouault was instinctively religious, although he was not always assiduous in religious practice. A Dominican father became his friend when he was about twenty; and among his close friends there have been a number of religious writers: Huysmans, Bloy, Suarès and Maritain. And certainly the horror and compassion which the first world war inspired in him had much to do with turning his imagination in a mystic direction. So it is not surprising that he should have distilled from his troubled emotions the poignant, haunting images of this volume which, as James Thrall Soby has observed in his comprehensive study of Rouault's work*, display the power and clarity of icons.

As to the burden of their meaning, their story, their message, naturally we first seek enlightenment in the captions or titles. Rouault has

---

* *Georges Rouault: Paintings and Prints.* James Thrall Soby. The Museum of Modern Art, New York, 1945.

changed them somewhat in the long course of the work. The final versions here reproduced he inscribed in his own hand especially for this edition. What are they? Passages of Scripture, some in Latin, some in French, fragments of Latin classics, a maxim of Pascal, certain popular proverbs which Rouault remembers his father quoting, and riddlesome questions and poetic fragments, more expressive than meaningful. Here and there one comes upon an explicit utterance referring to some protagonist: "Jean-François never sings allelulia . . ." (pl. 25). But the solution of the mystery of the work is not to be found in the accompanying words.

We turn the pages again. What do the pictures themselves tell us? Most familiar in the tradition of French art, and in Rouault's art, are images illustrative of the New Testament interspersed amid the other plates: Crown of Thorns, Ecce Homo, Mother of God, Veronica's Veil, Crucifixion, Resurrection. Some of the other imagery, though it does not contradict the religious symbolism, derives from more general regions of the artist's thought, and is not to be coordinated in words with anything theological. Here and there, in the reflections of Greek mythology (pl. 27, which seems to be Orpheus and his lyre) Rouault pays tribute to his beloved master, Gustave Moreau, who delighted in such subjects.

There is a mask which does not resemble Rouault, but bears some relation to other heads which he has presented as self-portraiture, a wistful, white-daubed clown (pl. 8); the caption is "Who does not paint himself a face?" There is a stooped, weary man with an immense bald brow, entitled "It is hard to live" (pl. 12). It shows the same deep compassion to be seen in the man condemned to death (pl. 18).

There are several women's heads. The first is specified to be a prostitute by that ironic appellation which is idiomatic in French: "Daughter of joy, so-called" (pl. 14). The next has a tragic face: "Mouth that was fresh, bitter as gall" (pl. 15). The third is a lady, complacent in her assurance of always enjoying some favoritism, even in heaven (pl. 16). The fourth is strange indeed: a sort of half-caste whom Rouault calls "affranchie," by which he means morally emancipated. Another is a decadently beautiful female figure, moping her life away (pl. 43). Another is a strangely helmeted woman in décolleté dress with a necklace, contemptuous of the follies of men. But with these we must consider the three representations of his feminine ideal, the Virgin and Child (pls. 13, 42, 56).

In Jean-François (pl. 25), one of the most beautiful plates, we come again to one of the essentials of Rouault's vision, a man of somewhat Asiatic aspect, whom he says he intended as the typical French sailor, risking his life in terrible foreign lands, famished and frightened. "Chinese invented gunpowder, they say, and made us a gift of it" (pl. 38) might be one of those suave, impenetrable merchants, peaceably dealing in death, world-wide. There is a naked man with a strained, neurotic attitude, "Are we not all convicts?" (pl. 6), and across the page there is a mad-looking creature, with a perhaps false crown and chain of office. Less strange are the German figures: plate 49 unmistakably caricatures the Kaiser Wilhelm II; plate 51, entitled "Far from the smile of Rheims" is both witty and pathetic; it represents a simple soldier with an eagle on his helmet, the iron cross on his breast, with professorial spectacles slipping half-way down his doleful face — the poor, good-hearted, culture-loving, law-abiding German, who nevertheless destroys cathedrals. And there are other satiric plates, decidedly contemporary in reference: a scene of fortune-telling which he observed during the first world war (pl. 41); and a pair of psychopathic characters (pl. 39).

All these images are fairly explicit; mordant and dramatic references to his own experience and current events and, again and again, his meditations on the Savior, his Christian inheritance. There are four superb plates of skeletons, standing in different attitudes, in powerful gesticulation. One may be taken as Death himself (pl. 36); others are only the pitiable dead, and in one there is a suggestion of the Day of Judgment (pl. 54).

Now let us try to see what all this signifies. As Rouault has said, "The least line or blur can instruct us more than any number of indigestible pamphlets" by means of that hierarchy and interior order which exist in art. Certainly the line or blur is subtler than the written word; it is an expression of a plurality of meaning. But without some oversimplification, which the artist himself may regret, we cannot exactly narrate his plot or sum up his message. Nevertheless the message seems to be: Man's fate upon earth is tragic. It is very hard for him to be sincere, and he inclines to traduce and mask himself in his relationships, male to female, man to man. As a rule his hope is folly. Look at plate 11, and read what is written there, "Tomorrow will be beautiful, said the shipwrecked man," as he sank into the sea. The everyday fate of man is to live by the sweat of his brow, never well enough. His love is in the subjunctive or in the future, never quite obtainable. Whole nations are predestined to hunger and thirst and fear, to invasion, devastation, displacement. The future is myth and mystery: a vague reign of alien potentates, misrule of paranoiacs, dance of death.

What shall man do? This great French artist feels that he is in the same plight as every man. Where can he turn? To the church, the Evangels, Jesus Christ dead and buried, risen the third day.

This is an epic without words; the story of an artist's implacable opposition to stupidity, his indignation at arrogance and brutishness, and his sympathy for fellow humanity. It is the *Comédie Humaine* of a great painter, the testimony of his own integrity maintained through solitude and sorrow.

PREFACE BY THE ARTIST

Here begins the preface of the artist to his work.

I dedicate this work to my master, Gustave Moreau, and also to my valiant and beloved mother who at the cost of extreme hardship facilitated my first endeavors at the crossroads where, as a young pilgrim very poorly endowed, I strayed. I should add that, although not of the same class, they both had the same smiling, encouraging kindliness, remote from the insolences and abuses which seem to prevail in these days.

The greater number of these subjects date from 1914 to 1918. They were first executed in the form of drawings in India ink, and later transformed into paintings in accordance with the wishes of Ambroise Vollard. He then had all the subjects transferred on to copper. It was desirable, apparently, that the copper should first receive the impression of my drawing. From that point on, I painstakingly tried to preserve the initial rhythm and draughtsmanship.

On each plate, more or less felicitously, without ceasing or pausing, I worked with different tools; there is no secret about my methods. Never satisfied, I resumed each subject endlessly, sometimes in as many as twelve or fifteen successive states; I should have liked them all to be of equal quality. I readily admit that I became attached to them, and that I was not insensitive to the desire of an American ambassador who wished to have some of the copper plates plated with gold and set in the wall at the embassy.

The impressions, which I carefully supervised, were completed in 1927, and later Ambroise Vollard had the plates cancelled.

After waiting twenty years for the appearance of this work which various circumstances delayed, I had the good fortune to recover the engravings in 1947, and was able to entrust the publication of the volume to the firm of L'Etoile Filante.

There had been some question of André Suarès' writing a text, but unfortunately he was unable to accomplish this.

The death of Ambroise Vollard, the war, the occupation and its consequences, and finally my lawsuit were all causes of indefinite delay. Notwithstanding a certain fundamental optimism, there were dark hours when I doubted that I should ever see the publication of this work, finished so long ago and always of the greatest importance in my opinion. I rejoice in the fact that I have reached my goal before I vanish from this planet.

If injustice has been shown Ambroise Vollard, let us agree that he had taste and a keen desire to make beautiful books without breaking any speed records, but it would have taken three centuries to bring to perfection the various works and paintings with which, in utter disregard of earthly limitations, he wished to burden the pilgrim.

Form, color, harmony
Oasis or mirage
For the eyes, the heart, and the spirit
Toward the moving ocean of pictorial appeal

"Tomorrow will be beautiful," said the shipwrecked man
Before he disappeared beneath the sullen horizon

Peace seems never to reign
Over this anguished world
Of shams and shadows

Jesus on the cross will tell you better than I,
Jeanne in her brief and sublime replies at her trial
As well as other saints and martyrs
Obscure or consecrated.

G.R.

Translated from the French by Monroe Wheeler

THE PLATES

1	Miserere mei, Deus, secundum magnam misericordiam tuam.	"Have mercy upon me, O God, according to Thy loving kindness." (*Psalms* 51:1)
2	Jésus honni . . .	Jesus reviled . . .
3	toujours flagellé . . .	eternally scourged
4	se réfugie en ton coeur, va-nu-pieds de malheur	take refuge in your heart, miserable vagabond
5	Solitaire, en cette vie d'embûches et de malices	Lonely sojourner in this life of pitfalls and malice
6	Ne sommes-nous pas forçats?	Are we not all convicts?
7	nous croyant rois	we think ourselves kings
8	Qui ne se grime pas?	Who does not paint himself a face?
9	Il arrive parfois que la route soit belle . . .	Sometimes the way is beautiful . . .
10	au vieux faubourg des Longues Peines	In the old suburb of Long-Suffering
11	Demain sera beau, disait le naufragé.	Tomorrow will be beautiful, said the shipwrecked man.
12	Le dur métier de vivre . . .	It is hard to live . . .
13	il serait si doux d'aimer	it would be so sweet to love
14	Fille dite de joie	Daughter of joy, so-called
15	En bouche qui fut fraîche, goût de fiel	Mouth that was fresh, bitter as gall
16	Dame du Haut-Quartier croit prendre pour le Ciel place réservée.	The society lady fancies she has a reserved seat in heaven.
17	Femme affranchie, à quatorze heures, chante midi	Emancipated woman, who has lost her way
18	Le condamné s'en est allé . . .	The condemned is led away . . .
19	son avocat, en phrases creuses, clame sa totale inconscience . . .	his lawyer, in hollow phrases, proclaims his entire unawareness . . .

20 sous un Jésus en croix oublié là	beneath a forgotten crucifix
21 "Il a été maltraité et opprimé et il n'a pas ouvert la bouche."	"He was oppressed, and he was afflicted, yet he opened not his mouth." (*Isaiah* 53:7)
22 En tant d'ordres divers, le beau métier d'ensemencer une terre hostile	In so many different ways, the noble vocation of sowing in hostile land
23 Rue des Solitaires	Street of the Lonely
24 "Hiver lèpre de la terre "	"Winter, leper of the earth"
25 Jean-François jamais ne chante alleluia . . .	Jean-François never sings allelulia . . .
26 au pays de la soif et de la peur	in the land of thirst and terror
27 Sunt lacrymae rerum . . .	"In all things, tears" (Virgil: *Aeneid I*)
28 "Celui qui croit en moi, fût-il mort, vivra."	"He that believeth in me, though he were dead, yet shall he live." (*John* 11:25)
29 Chantez Matines, le jour renaît	Sing matins, a new day is born.
30 "Nous . . . c'est en sa mort que nous avons été baptisés."	"Know ye not that so many of us as were baptized into Jesus Christ were baptized into his death." (*Romans* 6:3)
31 "Aimez-vous les uns les autres."	"That ye love one another." (*John* 13:34)
32 Seigneur, c'est vous, je vous reconnais.	Lord, it is Thou, I know Thee.
33 et Véronique au tendre lin passe encore sur le chemin . . .	and Veronica with her delicate linen still goes her way . . .
34 "Les ruines elles-mêmes ont péri."	"They have ruined even the ruins." (Lucian: *Pharcale IX,* 969)
35 "Jésus sera en agonie jusqu'à la fin du monde . . ."	"Jesus will be in anguish until the end of the world . . ." (Pascal: *Pensées*)
36 Ce sera la dernière, petit père!	This will be the last time, little father!
37 Homo homini lupus.	"Man is a wolf to man." (Plautus: *Asinaria* II, 4, 88)
38 Chinois inventa, dit-on, la poudre à canon, nous en fit don.	Chinese invented gunpowder, they say, and made us a gift of it.
39 Nous sommes fous.	We are insane.
40 Face à face	Face to face
41 Augures	Portents

42	Bella matribus detestata	"War, which all mothers hate" (Horace: *Odes I,* 1, 24-25)
43	"Nous devons mourir, nous et tout ce qui est nôtre."	"We all must die, we and all we possess." (Horace: *Ars Poetica,* 63)
44	Mon doux pays, où êtes-vous?	My sweet homeland, what has become of you?
45	La mort l'a pris comme il sortait du lit d'orties.	Death took him as he rose from his bed of nettles.
46	"Le juste, comme le bois de santal, parfume la hache qui le frappe."	"The righteous, like sandalwood, perfume the axe that falls on them."
47	"De profundis . . ."	"Out of the depths [have I cried unto thee, O Lord]." (*Psalms* 129:1)
48	Au pressoir, le raisin fut foulé.	In the press, the grapes were trodden.
49	"Plus le coeur est noble, moins le col est roide."	"The nobler the heart, the less stiff the collar."
50	"Des ongles et du bec "	"With tooth and nail" (Guillaume de Salluste: 1st week, 2nd day)
51	Loin du sourire de Reims	Far from the smile [of the angel] of Rheims
52	Dura lex sed lex.	The law is hard, but it is the law.
53	Vierge aux sept glaives	Virgin of the seven swords
54	"Debout les Morts!"	"Arise, ye dead!"
55	L'aveugle parfois a consolé le voyant.	Sometimes the blind have comforted those who see.
56	En ces temps noirs de jactance et d'incroyance, Notre-Dame de la Fin des Terres vigilante.	In these dark times of vainglory and unbelief, Our Lady of Land's End keeps vigil.
57	"Obéissant jusqu'à la mort et à la mort de la croix "	"Obedient unto death, even the death of the cross" (*Philippians* 2:8)
58	"C'est par ses meurtrissures que nous sommes guéris."	"And with his stripes we are healed" (*Isaiah* 53:5)

Pl. 1

Miserere mei, Deus,
secundum magnam misericordiam tuam.

Pl. 2

Jésus honni....

Pl. 3

toujours flagellé..

Pl. 4

se réfugie en ton cœur,
va-nu-pieds de malheur.

Pl. 5

Solitaire, en cette vie d'embûches
et de malices.

Pl. 6

Ne sommes-nous pas forçats?

Pl. 7

nous croyant rois.

Pl. 8

Qui ne se grime pas?

Pl. 9

Je arrive parfois que la route soit belle ....

Pl. 10

au vieux faubourg
des Longues Peines.

Pl. 11

Demain sera beau,
     disait le naufragé —

Pl. 12

Le dur métier de vivre...

Pl. 13

il serait si doux d'aimer.

Pl. 14

Fille dite de joie.

Pl. 15

En bouche qui fut fraîche, goût de fiel.

Pl. 16

Dame du Haut-Quartier croit prendre pour le Ciel place réservée.

Pl. 17

Femme affranchie,
à quatorze heures, chante midi.

Pl. 18

Le condamné s'en est allé...

Pl. 19

son avocat, en phrases creuses,
        clame sa totale inconscience...

Pl. 20

sous un Jésus en croix
oublié là.

Pl. 21

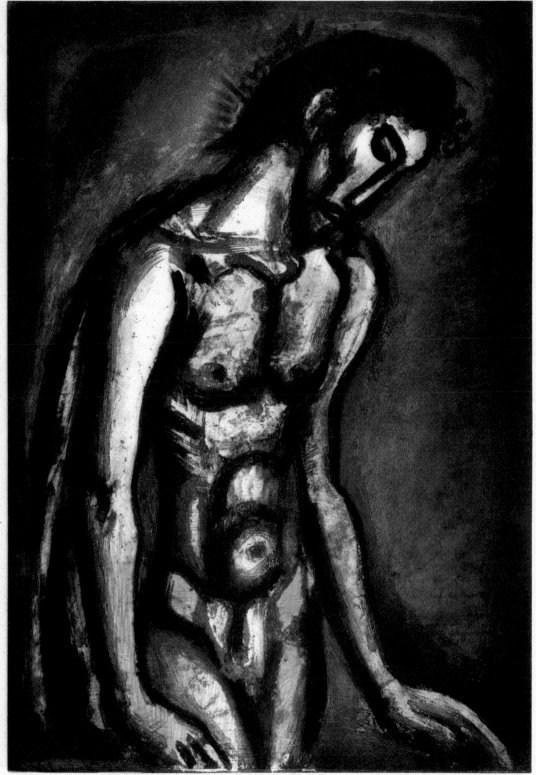

"Il a été maltraité et opprimé
et il n'a pas ouvert la bouche."

Pl. 22

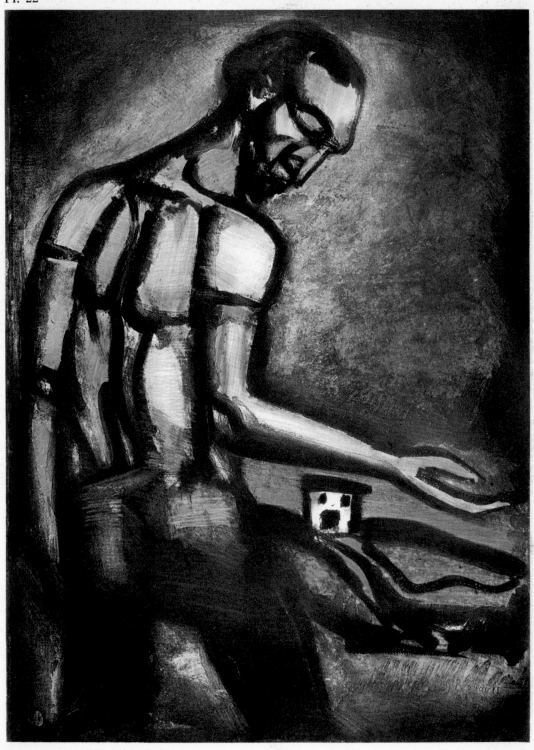

En tant d'ordres divers, le beau métier
d'ensemencer une terre hostile.

Pl. 23

Rue des Solitaires.

Pl. 24

"Hiver lèpre de la Terre."

Pl. 25

Jean-François jamais ne chante
alleluia...

Pl. 26

au pays de la soif et de la peur

Pl. 27

Sunt lacrymæ rerum...

Pl. 28

"Celui qui croit en moi,
fût-il mort, vivra."

Pl. 29

Chantez Matines, le jour renaît.

Pl. 30

"Nous... c'est en sa mort
que nous avons été baptisés."

Pl. 31

"Aimez-vous les uns les autres".

Pl. 32

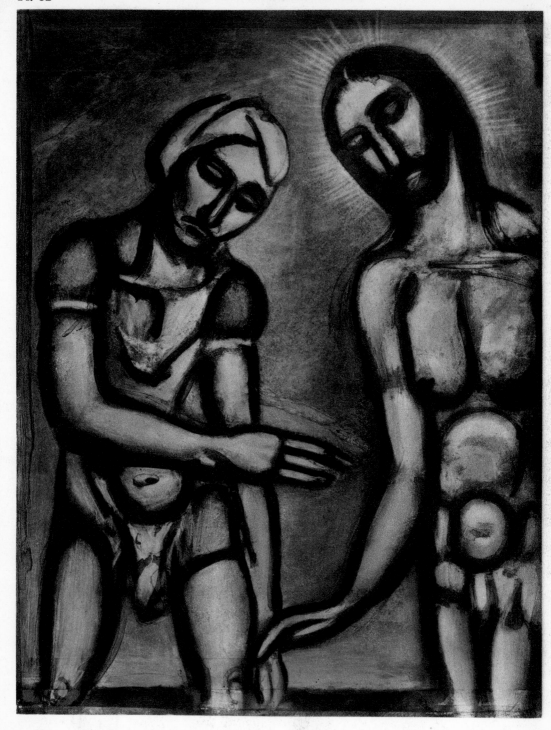

Seigneur, c'est vous,
je vous reconnais.

Pl. 33

et Véronique au tendre lin
   passe encore sur le chemin...

Pl. 34

"Les ruines elles-mêmes
ont péri."

Pl. 35

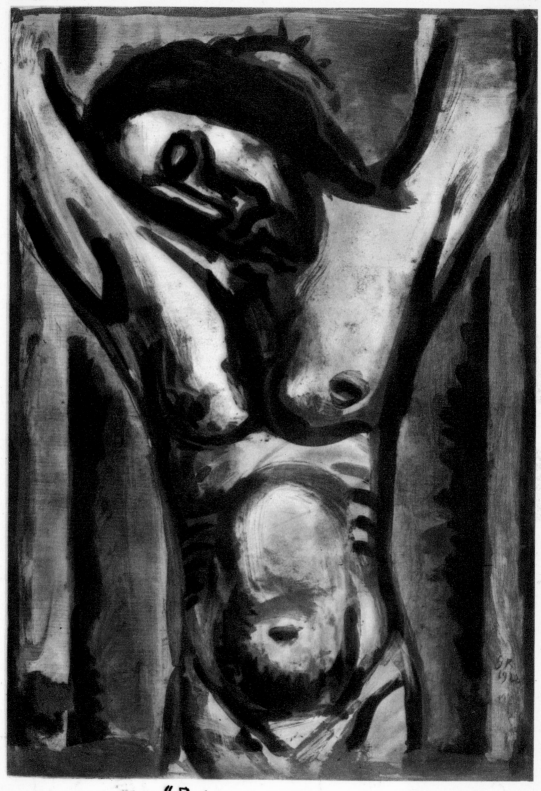

"Jésus sera en agonie
jusqu'à la fin du monde..."

Pl. 36

Ce sera la dernière, petit père!

Pl. 37

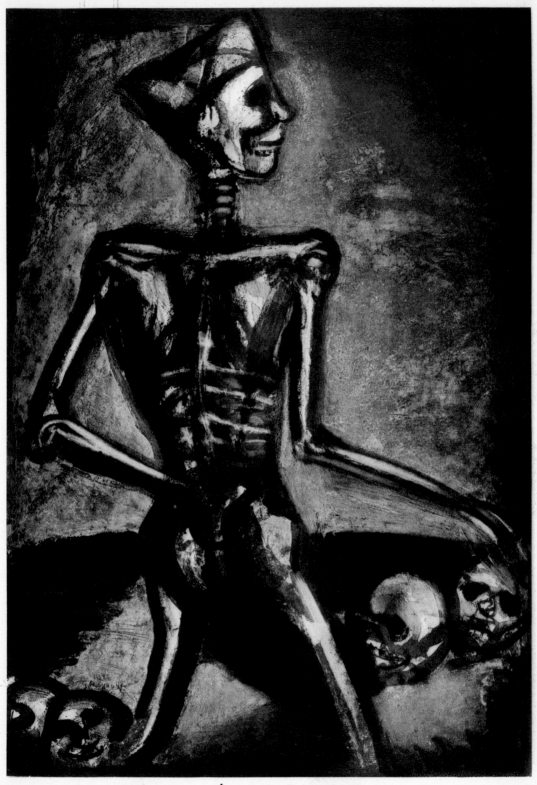

Homo homini lupus.

Pl. 38

Chinois inventa, dit-on,
la poudre à canon, nous en fit don.

Pl. 39

Nous sommes fous.

Pl. 40

Face à face.

Pl. 41

Augures.

Pl. 42

Bella matribus detestata.

Pl. 43

"Nous devons mourir,
      nous et tout'ce qui est nôtre."

Pl. 44

Mon doux pays, où êtes-vous?

Pl. 45

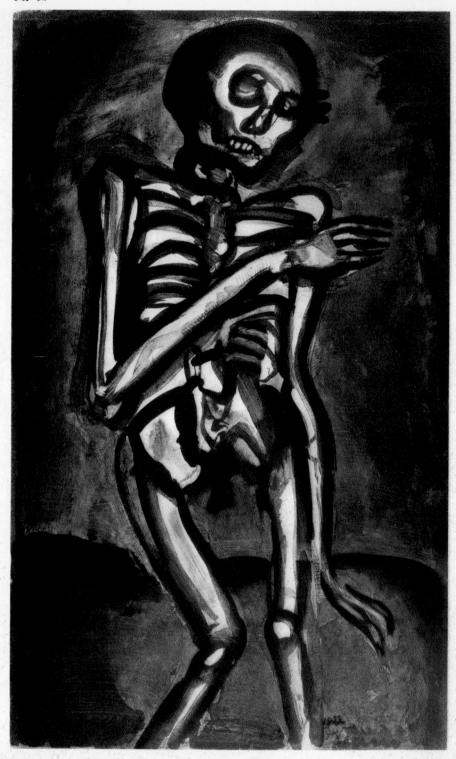

La mort l'a pris
comme il sortait du lit d'orties.

Pl. 46

"Le juste, comme le bois de santal,
parfume la hache qui le frappe."

Pl. 47

De profundis

Pl. 48

Au pressoir,
le raisin fut foulé.

Pl. 49

"Plus le cœur est noble,
        moins le col est roide."

Pl. 50

"Des ongles et du bec".

Pl. 51

Loin du sourire de Reims.

Pl. 52

Dura lex sed lex.

Pl. 53

Vierge aux sept glaives.

Pl. 54

"Debout les morts!"

Pl. 55

L'aveugle parfois a consolé le voyant.

Pl. 56

En ces temps noirs de jactance et d'incroyance,
Notre-Dame de la Fin des Terres vigilante.

Pl. 57

"Obéissant jusqu'à la mort et à la mort de la croix."

Pl. 58

"C'est par ses meurtrissures que nous sommes guéris."

Pl. 36 Various states of the same engraving, together with the final plate cancelled
Divers états successifs avec la planche définitive rayée.